LET'S TALK ABOUT SAFETY

19 WAYS YOU CAN WORK SAFELY

ANTON GUINEA

LET'S TALK ABOUT SAFETY
19 ways you can work safely

ISBN: 978-0-9806646-0-7
Author: Anton Guinea
Gladstone Queensland 4680 Australia
ABN: 83 116 111 543
www.letstalkaboutsafety.com.au
info@letstalkaboutsafety.com.au

First published by The Guinea Group of Companies Pty Ltd in 2009

The moral rights of the author have been asserted. The stories, suggestion and opinions of the author are personal views only. The strategies and steps outlined in this book may or may not be applicable to everyone.

Edited:
Crafted Expression www.craftedexpression.com.au

Design & Typesetting:
The Creative Collective www.thecreativecollective.com.au

Printed in China by:
Leverage Worldwide www.leverageworldwide.com

OTHER BOOKS BY ANTON

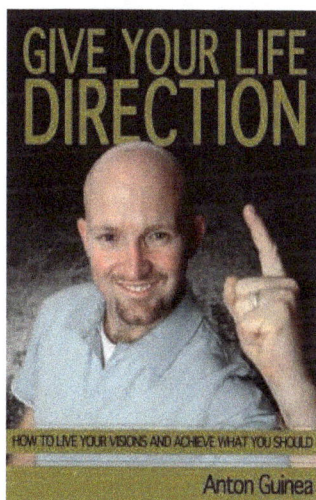

GIVE YOUR LIFE
DIRECTION

HOW TO LIVE YOUR VISIONS AND ACHIEVE WHAT YOU SHOULD

Anton Guinea

www.giveyourlifedirection.com.au

info@giveyourlifedirection.com.au

CONTENTS

Dedication 8

Foreword 9

Introduction 11

Chapter 1 13

Anton, I just don't have time to work safely;
we have to get the job done.

Chapter 2 16

Anton, I never follow procedure because
they're all wrong or not worth using.

Chapter 3 19

Anton, they always put production before safety here...
they say one thing, but do another.

Chapter 4 22

Anton, it won't happen to me. Look, I know how to
do my job. I've been doing it this way for years.

Chapter 5 25

Anton, safety is not my responsibility.
It is the company's responsibility.

Chapter 6 ....**28**

> Anton, I sometimes forget the importance
> of the choices I make at work.

Chapter 7 ....**31**

> Anton, I work safely, but
> my team members take risks.

Chapter 8 ....**34**

> Anton, if I get hurt, it won't matter;
> it'll only be me that suffers.

Chapter 9 ....**37**

> Anton, no matter what you do, you can't prevent
> accidents or incidents. Something will always happen.

Chapter 10 ....**40**

> Anton, it's just too much of a hassle to report a
> near-miss; you end up being treated like a criminal.

Chapter 11 ....**42**

> Anton, if I try to talk to my workmates about safety;
> they might tell me to 'bugger off'.

Chapter 12 ....**45**

> Anton, I only do 'safety stuff' because I have to,
> not because I want to, or because I see value in it.

Chapter 13 ....**48**

> Anton, I heard you had an incident at work.
> What happened?

Chapter 14 ....**52**

> Anton, my managers aren't serious about safety.
> They don't put enough time, energy, or resources into it.

Chapter 15 ....**55**

> Anton, the only reason we have safety systems around here
> is because the managers want to cover their arse.

Chapter 16 ....**58**

> Anton, if I work safely, my team members
> think I'm stupid and ridicule me.

Chapter 17 ....**61**

> Anton, it's great when I have to do some work
> at home; I don't have to do all the safety stuff, I
> can just hop in and get it done!

Chapter 18 ....**63**

> Anton, where to from here? How can i apply.
> some of the things we've been discussing?

Chapter 19 ....**65**

> Anton, thanks for the chat. How else can I
> apply the information we've discussed?

Safety Belief Busters..**68**

> How to break away from those old safety beliefs

Thanks and acknowledgements **70**

> Without you all, this would not be possible

About the author..**72**

Bibliography **76**

DEDICATIONS

To all those workers that have ever had a workplace incident or accident and have suffered due to an error of judgment, of their own or of others, I dedicate this book to you. It is a tragedy to be involved in any workplace incident; the pain and suffering of injured workers causes grief and sorrow to their families all over the world.

As always, to my dear wife, Julie, who was one of the first people to arrive at the hospital on the day that I was injured at work. She suffered through my period in intensive care, then when I was in the Burns Unit in Brisbane. Julie is a champion and my life would be so much less without her. Toby and Zac are growing up and know how important it is to stay safe in life. Had the unthinkable happened on that Tuesday morning in March, 1994, they would never have been born.

FOREWORD

By Marc McLaren

Anton is not just passionate about safety, he lives it 24/7; no-one should be hurt while doing their job. He is a person of immense integrity and this book is like its writer; it is truly motivational and speaks to the heart.

Let's Talk About Safety draws together two powerful and life changing safety ideas. In a plain English manner Anton explains that our beliefs, what we hold to be true about safety, drive our behaviours and that real conversations in the workplace can infl uence our safety beliefs. It does this in a passionate and personal manner, moving us beyond mere safety theory to life saving thinking and actions.

The big questions about safety are tackled honestly and head on by Anton. In a down to earth and refreshing style, the person at the "front line" to the senior manager is challenged to reconsider what they believe in and to rethink their approach to safety.

This book will get you in from the very first page and I guarantee you won't be able to put it down until you have finished reading it.

Let the safety revolution begin and remember it takes only one genuine safety discussion to potentially save a life and change a whole organisation's approach to safety. This book needs to get into the hands of every person in your organisation, regardless of whether they see are a reader or not.

Beware in picking up this book it may change the way you think about safety, the choices you make about safety and the conversations you have with others about safety.

Marc McLaren
Safety4Life Executive Manager

INTRODUCTION

G'day mate, my name is Anton Guinea. How's things? Thanks for taking the time today to discuss your beliefs and feelings about safety.

I began work as an Apprentice Electrician at Queensland Alumina in Gladstone, Queensland. From there, I moved to Western Australia, where I worked on an Iron Ore mine in Pannawonica. I have also worked on a Uranium Mine, and in a Copper Smelter.

I have been around safety for a long time now and my present work sometimes takes me to sites and companies like yours to discuss safety with employees and managers.

I can still remember when I was a first year apprentice, the Electrical Workshop Supervisor announced one day that we were going to start having 'safety meetings'. "I am not sure what they are" he said, "but we have been told to have them once a week". That was in 1990 and a lot has happened in safety since then, particularly in the attitudes of workers to safety and how they view not only the process, but their own role in workplace safety. The role of managers in the safety process is also an interesting topic for discussion.

One of the most important things worth knowing about safety is that your beliefs, your values and your attitudes towards safety have a direct influence on your behaviours.

That is, if you believe that safety is a waste of time, or that you don't have time to work safely, that is how you will act. Your beliefs drive your behaviours. That is why it is so important to examine and understand what you believe about safety. And yes, it is possible to change your beliefs and attitudes; you have to want to do that, though.

At the end of our discussion, why don't you commit to taking some action? Why don't you set a goal to do something to improve safety on site? You might like to set a safety choice goal (or goals) on the page provided at the back of the book.

Now, let's discuss some of the things that are bugging you, and don't be afraid to be completely honest with me ...

CHAPTER 1

> **Anton, I just don't have time to work safely; we have to get the job done.**

Mate, you don't have the time not to work safely. You must remember that it is part of your job to work safely and exercise a duty of care to yourself and others. Then, you also need to think about how much time you will need to recover after a serious incident.

This belief can be formed when you feel that it is important to spend more time on the job, not doing safety paperwork. Sometimes it feels like the paperwork is a waste of time. Let me assure you that the time you spend on the safety aspects of the job are as important as the time that you spend on the job itself.

The thing about it is that safety is part of your job, and it is not your own time that you are taking to work safely. You are getting paid to do it. The boss knows that jobs take a bit longer now than they used to, given that you need to get your permits and do a safety analysis or a risk assessment of the job before you even begin. It is so important that you do these things, as they may just save you from getting hurt. If you notice only one thing in your safety analysis or risk assessment that may prevent you, or your workmates, from being injured, then the time put into safety has been well spent.

When you think about what is at stake, why wouldn't you take an extra ten minutes, or even an hour, to make sure you cover all your bases? If the time that it takes you to do the job safely has not been factored into the job, then tell someone – the planner or the supervisor – because if they don't know that a job takes longer because you need to do it safely, they can never allocate the correct time to get the job done.

If the boss has a go at you for taking too long, don't be put off. Just explain that you are taking the time to do it safely, so you don't get hurt. Do what ever it takes to do the job safely and if you are honest and up-front with the boss, he or she should understand.

Mate, I understand that you have to get the job done, but at what cost? You know, it is amazing how many people get hurt at work each year - mostly because they have not taken the time to work safely. If getting the job done means you putting yourself at risk, then my advice is: "Don't do it. Find another way to do the job." It is that simple, really. Although you think you are saving time by taking a short cut, or rushing to get the job done, just imagine what could happen if you were to get hurt.

I know from experience that it takes much longer to recover, than to do the job safely. Just imagine some of the injuries that you could sustain on your job, and think about how long you could be out of work for and how long you would continue to suffer the pain. You may never fully recover, and in many years time, you may be wishing that you took just that little bit longer to do that job. I know plenty of people who think just like that.

> " *So, mate, you really don't need to rush that job. It will take you a lot longer to recover than it will to do it safely now.* "

CHAPTER 2

> ❝ *Anton, I never follow procedures because they're all wrong or they're not worth using.* ❞

Mate, you are crazy! Safety procedures are not designed to make it diffi cult for you, they are not designed to make the job take longer, and they are not designed to create obstacles to you getting your work done. Procedures are developed as the safest way to do the job. Procedures are developed with one objective; to keep you safe.

This belief, that the procedures are wrong or worthless, can be formed if you continually see that procedures are outdated, you feel that you were not part of the procedure development process or you were not consulted about the implementation of the procedure.

If the procedures are outdated, what have you done about it, mate? You know your job better than anyone and if the procedures need to be updated, have you taken steps to get the changes made? Sometimes it can be easier to whinge about them not being correct, than to actually do something about getting the procedures updated.

It is important to remember that the expectation is that you will follow safe work procedures on every job. If you do not, you really need a good reason why, because the boss thinks the procedure is up-to-date and is the safest way to do the job. In your situation, I would get in fi rst, and raise the issue with the boss.

If you just don't see a good reason to follow procedures, you might like to think about why that is: is it because you have been doing the job in the same way for the last however-many years; or is it because you just can't understand how someone in an offi ce could write a procedure that tells you how to do your job; or is it because you think there is a better, maybe even safer, way to do the job? Remember, even if you are doing the job in an even safer way than the procedure dictates, you are still taking a short cut if you are not following the procedure – you may reduce your own risk, but what about your mates on the same shift or on the next shift? Perhaps you could let them know how they could work safer – they will certainly appreciate the information, if it will make them and their jobs safer.

If you have a reason not to follow procedures, you need to think it through, to be sure that your reason is valid. Perhaps you are just being stubborn and the procedure is the best way to do the job, but you have an issue with it because you don't like someone telling you how to do your job.

> " *So mate, always remember that safety procedures were put in place to keep you safe. If you find a safer way to do the job, update the procedure.* "

CHAPTER 3

> ❝ **Anton, they always put production before safety here... they say one thing, but do another.** ❞

Mate, it might appear that way. But you have to remember two things: firstly, the company relies on its output, which you and your workmates are paid to produce. Secondly, it is always your choice, and if you allow production to be put before your own safety, believe me, it is you and your loved ones who will suffer most.

This belief, that the company puts production before safety, arises from seeing the company continually focusing on production and output, and not listening to your ideas about safety. So it might appear that the company won't adopt safety measures for fear that production will suffer.

Looking at the issue from the production perspective, you are paid to do your job in the most productive manner possible, but you are also expected to keep yourself and your workmates safe; that is, you will not allow production or other priorities to get in the way of you doing your job safely. Whenever you feel as though you are being pressured to put other priorities before your own safety, you need to remember who has most to lose. Mate, you need to stand up and say something; you need to make people aware that you are feeling pressured and uncomfortable with what is being asked of you. Ultimately, the choices you make are your responsibility alone – no-one can make you do something that you are not comfortable doing.

If the boss is putting the pressure on you to put production, or some other goal, before safety, they may not realise they are asking you to put yourself in an unsafe position. That is why you begin to think that, while they always preach safety, their actions don't support it. But if the boss is not even aware that they are pressuring you, it is your responsibility to let them know how you are feeling, and that your primary focus is your own safety. That usually works.

However, if you boss is one of the few who really just don't care about employee safety, and are concerned only about productivity, then you have a problem. Nevertheless, you are responsible for the choices you make – you cannot be forced to do something that is unsafe. In that situation, you may need to have a frank and forthright discussion with the boss – a discussion that may save you an injury. The boss needs to understand that productivity will be seriously affected if you, or one of your workmates, gets hurt at work. It is in the company's best interest for you not to get injured, as they will need to recover the situation, which takes time; they will have to attend to your needs, and they will have to justify their actions.

Also, some of the pressure that you are feeling might not be from the boss but from within you – an eagerness to get the work done so that the boss thinks you are doing a good job. Be careful of perceived pressure, as this can be something that alters your judgement at critical moments, too.

> " *So mate, nothing comes before your safety, and if it seems like it does, it may not be real pressure, only perceived. Always make sure you put your safety first.* "

CHAPTER 4

❝ *Anton, it won't happen to me...* ❞
Look, I know how to do my job.
I've been doing it this way for years.

Mate, I cannot believe you think that. Who do you think gets hurt at work every day of every year? People just like you, who thought, just like you, that they knew their jobs so well that they could never come to any harm. Unfortunately, that is not the way it works.

The belief that it won't happen to you can be formed when you have had a working life free of major incidents.

But if you don't examine your work practices regularly to be sure that they are safe, you may become a victim of a workplace incident even though you have a long incident-free record.

Safety incidents and injuries do not discriminate; older workers with years of experience get injured at work as frequently as the young and inexperienced. The only real thing that determines whether or not employees get hurt is their decision to work safely or to ignore safety.

Yes, it may never happen to you, provided you understand that your approach to workplace safety is the key determining factor. If you think you will never get hurt at work, you are more like to take risks and to take shortcuts, rather than making the choice to work safely. If you can change your mindset and acknowledge that others doing the same job as you have been injured, sometimes permanently, then you will start to open your mind up to the possibilities of what could go wrong around you. You will start to be mindful of the hazards of your job, and you will take steps to limit those hazards before starting work.

If you still think that you will never get hurt because you know your job so well, think again. Sometimes, it can be complacency which causes you to be unaware of the hazards in your job. Complacency is working on 'autopilot' and not noticing what is going on around you. That you have always done your job in a particular way without incident does not mean that there cannot be a safer way to do it. Be willing to listen to the ideas of others, as they may have just found a safer, perhaps even more effi cient, way to do that job. Stand back and think objectively about the way you do your job; assess if it is the safest way that it could possibly be done. I bet you could make some improvements and make the job safer. If you do, why not share it with everyone so that they can benefit, too.

> " Mate, don't think it will never happen to you, because safety does not discriminate. The only thing that will save you from getting hurt is working safely. "

CHAPTER 5

❝ *Anton, safety is not my* ❞ *responsibility; it is the company's responsibility.*

Mate, it still surprises me that I hear people say that. You are only one of many employees who still think that it is their supervisor's, or their manager's, or even the Site Safety Officer's responsibility to keep them safe. Mate, there is only one person responsible for your safety, and that is you.

The mistaken belief that workplace safety is not your responsibility can form because it is so much easier to leave

*the company in charge of safety, to shrug off responsibility
and disengage from the process.*

I just cannot understand why anyone would trust their safety
to their boss. If something happens to you, yes, the boss will
have to explain it to your family, the company will have to
take responsibility, but it will be you laid up and in pain. It is
your family that will suffer the loss of their security.

Your primary responsibility is to refuse to allow anything
to compromise your safety. Don't allow any other
considerations, such as productivity, or even people in the
company, to convince you to work in an unsafe manner.
Take a stand and be responsible for your actions and your
decisions.

You might even think about more than just taking
responsibility for your own safety - the safety of others.
You should ensure that your workmates are aware of your
attitude to workplace safety; explain that it is you that
will get injured if something goes wrong, and that you
are unwilling to make unsafe choices. Your actions speak
louder than words, and by being safety-conscious you
are not only changing your own behaviour, but you may
also be changing the behaviour of others thereby making
a real difference to those around you. Remember that
your workmates are watching you and assessing from your
actions, how you feel about working safely; if you are a risk
taker or a short cutter, be assured that your workmates will
decide that if it is good enough for you, it is good enough
for them. By taking responsibility for your own safety, and the
safety of those around you, you will increase the chances

that you will all go home from work in the same condition that you arrived.

By taking responsibility, you can rest assured that you have done everything in your power to prevent yourself from being injured. Also, while you will never know if you have saved a life, you can be sure that you have also done everything in your power to make the job safer for those around you.

> *So mate, it is no-one else's responsibility for your safety but your own. By taking responsibility you will prevent an injury to yourself, and you might even be an example for others.*

CHAPTER 6

> **" Anton, I sometimes forget the importance of the choices that I make at work. "**

Mate, that is easy to do. So let me suggest that you always need to remember what happened to James Wood.

James was born in Scotland in December 1962, the eldest of six children, of a stay-at-home mum and an underground coal miner dad. At the age of 15, James commenced work as an Apprentice Diesel Mechanic in an underground coal mine, where he learnt the skills required to maintain heavy earth moving equipment. James completed his trade at the age of 19 and continued to work at the mine. After four years as a tradesman, James's life was great: he was enjoying his work and he was discussing marriage and the future with his high school sweetheart.

And then, the unthinkable happened. Just before his 'smoko' break, one morning in September 1985, James completed a fan belt replacement on a mine truck and was asked to relocate the truck to another area of the mine. As he drove it down a damp haul road, the truck rolled three times. James, who was not wearing a seat belt, was thrown from the cab, through the open driver's side window. As he landed, he broke several bones is his spine and damaged his spinal cord. He has not walked since.

James spent the next three months in a spinal ward. It took more than six weeks for the bones in his back to heal, and during that time not only was he not allowed to move at all, but he even had to go to the toilet lying in bed. In his words, "that was by far the toughest time of the recovery – not moving for over six weeks was a huge mental struggle". After leaving hospital, James spent six months in a rehabilitation home, where he learnt to adapt to his new life in a wheel-chair. He explains this period by saying that "I had to learn to live again – everything changes, not only the way that I got around, but the way that I dressed myself, the way I used the toilet and every other aspect of my life."

James takes full responsibility for his accident, and he knows that the fact that he cannot walk is due primarily to the choice he made that day to not wear a seat belt. He can no longer do things that most of us take for granted. At the time of his accident, James was not a safety-focussed worker, he let the views of other people cloud his judgement and suffered an unbelievable tragedy because he failed to take responsibility for his own safety.

Finally, and perhaps most importantly, James's core belief is that prevention is better than cure. He urges people to take responsibility and make safe choices, both at work and in life. James is now a motivational safety speaker, and if the responses from his audiences are anything to go by, people defi nitely heed his message.

Just think of James Wood and you will remember to make safe choices at work.

Here are some photos of James now. Since his incident, James has represented Australia at both the Para Olympics and the world championships for wheel-chair racing.

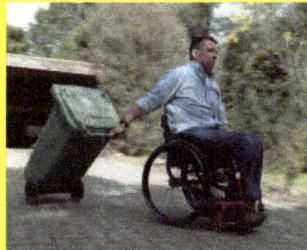

CHAPTER 7

> **Anton, I work safely, but my team members take risks.**

Mate, in that case, you again have two options. The first is to take responsibility for your own safety, and make sure that you do what it takes to avoid incident or injury. The second is to approach your workmates and have a frank discussion with them about their actions.

This might not even be just a belief – this may be a real situation. Also, if you have noticed your workmates taking risks, it may be useful to consider that they may be thinking the same thing about you …

The challenge you face is that the actions of others can impact on your safety; the way that others work can directly determine whether or not you will go home to your family at the end of your shift or roster. The fact that things totally out of your control can change in your work area means that those around you have a degree of responsibility for your safety, as well as their own.

If you take the fi rst option, to take responsibility for your safety only, this is called working independently. It means that you will follow procedures and be mindful of workplace safely. However, it also means that you will only take action to make the workplace safer if it impacts on you – if the risk or the hazard affects someone else, you will take no responsibility for that situation, or the outcomes.

A second option, the most desirable, is to work interdependently. If you are interdependent, you will try and change the views of your workmates, you will try to convince them that working safely will prevent everyone from having an incident or an injury. This is a worthwhile option but a tough one that will test your courage. Nevertheless, it is worth having the discussion if your work mates if they are making the workplace unsafe for you; you may be able to work with them to see how they can change their behaviour and make the workplace safer for everyone.

The third and least desirable option is to be a dependant worker. This is where you give all the responsibility for your safety to the company. You make yourself dependant on them to provide everything for you, from direction, to supervision, to systems and procedures. This is obviously not a safe way to work. Being dependant means that you are not mindful of the risks and hazards around you, that you will wait for someone else, or the company, to control them and prevent you from being injured.

> **"** *So mate, look after yourself, but do remember that the actions of your workmates affect your safety. Take the interdependent approach and ask them to consider your safety, as well as theirs.* **"**

The information in this chapter is adapted from 'The Bradley Curve'. More information can be found on the Bradley Curve at: http://telsafe.org/Documents/The%20Bradley%20Curve.pdf.

CHAPTER 8

> **Anton, if I get hurt, it won't matter; it'll only be me that suffers.**

Mate, nothing could be further from the truth. It is amazing, though, how many employees have this view. When they are at work, they think it is alright to take a risk or two, as it is only them that will be injured. And that maybe true – if no-one else is close enough to be affected by your unsafe actions, only you may be injured. But that is where only hurting yourself ends.

This belief is an easy one to acquire. Sometimes, and I have done this while trying to get a job done, you forget that there are many people who love you, and who would be shattered if you were injured.

When you are injured at work, the company contacts your next of kin right away. That is why you supply your emergency contact details when you commence your employment. So your mother, father, signifi cant other, siblings and friends are the first to know. They may not be provided with all the information about your incident or injuries, they will panic and worry about what awaits them at the hospital or medical centre.

This is where the pain starts for your loved ones, those people that you did not consider when you decided to take that shortcut. That shortcut was supposed to save you a few minutes, but now, on your way to the hospital, you may just have started the rest of your life. Your family is now left to deal with the aftermath of the tragedy – they might have to bathe and feed you, or just sit patiently with you while you recover. It is your loved ones who will have to take up the burden of the work that you use to do around home, playing with the kids and being a loving supporting partner.

When you are at work, and are next considering whether or not to take a risk, imagine that your family is standing beside you asking you to work safely so that you can go home to them to continue to live a blessed life. Imagine that in that moment, you can change the course of your life for the better, by minimising the risk of harming yourself. The choice for safety is a choice to make life better for your loved ones, as well as yourself.

" So mate, always consider who you are really hurting when you choose to take a safety shortcut at work. It might be only you that gets injured, but it is your loved ones that will really suffer. "

CHAPTER 9

> **" Anton, no matter what you do, you can't prevent accidents or incidents; something will always happen. "**

Mate, didn't you just tell me in Chapter 4 that it will never happen to you? So, what you are saying is that accidents and injuries are going to happen, but it won't be you that gets hurt – in your workplace, shit happens, just not to you.

This belief forms if you are not open to incident prevention. Each year a large number of people are injured at work and the investigations show that the vast majority of those could have, and should have, been prevented.

Generally, the workplaces where shit happens have a culture of shortcutting and risk taking, as well as a lack of support for safety systems and a lack of focus on the role of employees in making the workplace safe. Safety culture is the term used to describe 'the way we do things around here'. If a company has a 'poor' safety culture, it means that the employees tend to make decisions about the way to do their work that could cause them to be injured.

Shit doesn't just happen; there is always a reason for it. It is proven that almost all workplace incidents are caused by human behaviour and poor safety choices. Employees can take control, they can choose, and they can take responsibility for creating a safer workplace.

Employees regularly tell me that "accidents will always happen here, that is the mining game" or "if you hang around long enough, you will see someone hurt or killed" or, even worse "it is only a matter of time until someone gets hurt or killed here – it is the nature of our work". The problem with these comments, and the mindset that generates them, is that thoughts have a way of transforming into actions and outcomes. What you believe will happen, is most likely what will happen. It may happen to you, or to someone that you know and love, or someone you have worked with for many years.

When you believe that incidents will just happen, you don't bother to take the time or make the effort to work safely.

It is important to understand that incidents and injuries are preventable. There are organisations, such as DuPont, that have operated for extended lengths of time without an incident. It is possible to stop shit from happening, but it takes effort and commitment from everyone. Most importantly, employees have to believe that it is possible not to hurt anyone, and to act in a way that is not only safe, but is focused on prevention.

> *So mate, accidents and incidents don't just happen, they are caused, and if they are caused, they are preventable. Will you do your bit to prevent incidents from occurring?*

CHAPTER 10

> *Anton, it's just too much of a hassle to report a near miss; you end up being treated like a criminal.*

Mate, I know the feeling - it has happened to me in the past. I remember reporting an issue with the test track for haul trucks on the mine site that I worked on in Western Australia. I was told that "I was just causing trouble" and that "if no-one got hurt, it couldn't be that big of an issue". That really put me off reporting near misses. Fortunately, no-one was ever hurt on that test track, and I would have felt terrible if there had been an incident.

It is common for employees not to want to report near misses. They might feel that they are 'dobbing' on workmates and after all, who wants to cause trouble over something that didn't hurt anyone. Or, they don't want to cause trouble over something that no-one really needs to know about, because what will the boss say when he or she has to complete all that paper work? Then, of course, there will be the investigation, which might point the blame at the employee who reported the problem and cause the employee to be disciplined in some way.

None of these things may happen. But regardless of what comes out of the report or the investigation, it is imperative that near misses are not only reported, but also investigated, because without investigation, hazards remain and someone might get hurt.

Near misses are both early warning signs and they are free kicks, so to speak, because no-one was injured. The most important thing about near misses is that recurrences can be prevented if they are reported and if action is taken. By reporting near misses, you might just be saving yourself or your workmates from being hurt. The company does not want to discipline you for reporting near misses; it wants to learn from them. It wants to do things better, and safer. Also, the more near misses that the company has, the closer it is getting to a major incident (even a fatality).

> **So mate, just report near misses. You can potentially save someone from injuring themselves. The company only wants to learn from them.**

CHAPTER 11

> **" Anton, if I try to talk to "**
> **my workmates about safety, they**
> **might tell me to "bugger off".**

Let me get this straight, Mate. You were in the workshop last week, when you noticed one of your workmates working in an unsafe manner and you did not approach him to talk about safety because you were afraid they would tell you to bugger off?

If you truly care about your workmates, it should not be hard to approach them and tell them that you are worried about their safety and their well-being. If one of your children was doing something unsafe, like not wearing a seat belt or riding a bike without a helmet, you would defi nitely say something, wouldn't you. That is because you care so much about your children.

I understand your fear that the response will be hostile, because that has happened to me when I have had safety discussions with employees in different companies. When you think about it, though, a hostile reaction is just that. It is the way the person has reacted in the moment. They might become verbally aggressive, but they are unlikely to be violent. In that case you simply walk away knowing that you have done all that you could to prevent an incident or an injury to your workmate.

In fact, though, it is very rare that people get aggressive when you talk to them about working safely. Most companies have worked hard to ensure that employees know that they are responsible for talking about safety with their workmates, and it is almost an expectation that they will.

If the person reacts in a way that is supportive and obliging, you will have the opportunity to hold a meaningful safety discussion and share your ideas and views. You might even learn something about the job that they are doing. And, more importantly, you might prevent an incident from occurring – you might even save someone's life. And you will certainly be able to walk away with a clear conscience, knowing that you had the courage, and cared enough, to make a difference. You were able to put your fear aside and approach someone and meaningfully discuss how they could be safer at work. You should be congratulated.

> **"** *So mate, it is not so hard after all. Just try to have a meaningful safety discussion and see how it goes. Then, keep at it, and you will get better at it, and you will help keep your workmates and workplace safe.* **"**

CHAPTER 12

> **Anton, I only do 'safety stuff' because I have to, not because I want to do it, or because I see value in it.**

Mate, so what you are telling me is that you are just complying with what you have to do, just going through the motions. You don't really take any interest in the safety systems (such as job safety analysis or risk assessments for example); you follow them only because the boss or the company says that you have to.

The belief that safety is just another thing that you have to do is easy to form. Safety can be both very prescriptive and repetitive and can become mundane. You can easily start to believe that you just have to comply with what the company wants, rather than actively engaging in the process.

The problem is that when you are in compliance mode, you are not being proactive. You are not taking responsibility for your own safety. You might think that you are working safely, and that you don't need all of that paperwork to do your job properly. You may even tell yourself that you do all the 'safety stuff' in your head. You have never had an incident and you can't see why you need to write anything down.

All of that might be true, but safety systems are not designed to make it difficult for you, they are designed to prompt you to think about the job and they are designed to get you to spend a few minutes at the start of the job planning how you are going to do it safely. They are designed to prompt you to look around and identify and analyse any risks or hazards that might make the job unsafe. When you have identified the hazards, you can plan to control them.

Only if you are using the safety systems properly will you be sufficiently focused to identify and control hazards. If you are using systems as they are designed to be used, and with a positive attitude, they will deliver value.

It is important that you view safety systems as value adding tools that assist you to do your job safely. It is easy to fall into the trap of being compliant, though, as you are expected to follow the processes every single day. And you are expected to follow them even for the simple jobs that you have done 100 times before. Don't forget that the safety systems are designed to help you to avoid complacency, and to help you to think about how you can work more safely. The more that you engage in using the safety systems, the more benefi t you will derive from them.

> **So mate, don't just be compliant, be committed to the safety processes.**

CHAPTER 13

**❝ Anton, I heard that you had ❞
an incident at work. What happened?**

Mate, I did have an incident because of my mistaken beliefs about safety. I was 21, and I believed that I was invincible.

I had completed my Electrical Apprenticeship and was trade qualified, but there was no work around back then, and I had to take a role as a Trades Assistant to an Electrician.

On a Tuesday morning in March, 1994, the Electrician and I were given the job of mounting overload blocks in a number of switchboards. It was a fairly simple job, the plant was in shutdown mode, and there was no rush to get the job completed. We had isolated the required switchboards and had tested that they were de-energised. We had followed all of the safety processes on that site, and we had obtained a work permit to do the job. We had completed the safety requirements and other preparation and could now get to work.

What happened next was totally unexpected. The first switchboard that we started working on blew up – it quite literally erupted in my face, sending out a ball of flame that engulfed the top half of my body and threw me backwards onto the floor of the substation. In that instant, I had suffered second degree burns, and was to spend the next three days in intensive care, before spending most of the next month in the burns unit in Brisbane.

The switchboard blew up because I had used a steel ruler to measure where we would be mounting the overload blocks. That the switchboard was isolated and tested to be dead did not matter, because the steel ruler was thin enough to slide in behind the main switch and touch live conductors that I should not have been able to contact.

While I was lying in intensive care, the General Manager of the site came up to hospital to tell me that I should not worry about what had happened; the investigation has started and had established that we had followed all of the required safety procedures; we had done nothing wrong. Well then, why had I been hurt so badly, almost killed, and why was I lying in intensive care?

Simply because we had followed all of the safety processes only because we had to. We had not taken a few minutes to stand back and consider how to do the job more safely. I had chosen to use a steel ruler in a switchboard and we had chosen not to isolate the entire cubicle before starting work.

My first book, 'Give Your Life Direction' provides a more detailed overview of the incident.

Here is a photo of what one of my hands looked life following the burns (both hands and my face looked the same). The skin had to be forcibly removed with tweezers to 'promote new skin growth', holy macanoli that was painful. There is a photo of me presenting a safety session to workers in Townsville, Queensland and our family and friends during a recent trip to Tasmania.

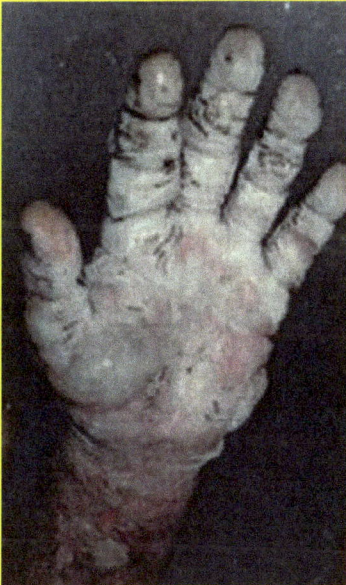

CHAPTER 14

> **Anton, my managers are not serious about safety. They don't put enough time, energy or resources into it.**

Mate, I know it often seems like that. Managers ask you to look for hazards and issues in the workplace, and then when you report them, they never fix them, or never tell you what is happening or what is planned. And they often comment on the cost of making the necessary repairs or modifications. The message you receive is that the company is not committed to safety.

This belief arises when you don't see action being taken by managers to rectify safety concerns. Remember, though, you may not see what is happening behind the scenes.

What is actually happening is that the company is committed to understanding where the hazards lie in your workplace, and they want you to be part of the solution and identify them, so that action can be taken. Once identifi ed, hazards are recorded and responsibility is assigned to someone in the company to attend to the safety issue or concern. If you don't see any action in regard to the safety issues that you have raised, you may like to follow it up and ask questions of the responsible people. It should be easy enough to fi nd them, but you have to be willing to go looking for answers.

What is probably happening is that the company is allocating budget funds to fixing the issue. The challenge for companies is that they are running a business and they need to authorise and approve funding for safety, just like they have to approve it for maintenance or operations. Generally, there is a substantial budget allocated to fixing safety issues, so it should not take too long to get funding approval. The next step is to obtain and review quotes for the work and finally to plan the repairs or work necessary. These also take time, so as you can see, the process of attending to safety issues can take a little while. That does not mean that nothing is happening.

But sometimes the safety issue might even be something that you can take care of right now, instead of you having to go through the process of reporting it and waiting for something to happen. You are able to make it so much easier for the boss when you take safely solutions, not safety issues, to him or her. The boss sees that you are committed to the safety process and your commitment will win you their support when you next need it in relation to a job taking longer to complete in order to do it safely or when another safety issue needs to be attended to and you are unable to address the issue yourself.

> " *So mate, management is taking action on the issues you raise. You might even be able to fix some issues yourself, or at least track the progress of the issues that you have raised.* "

CHAPTER 15

> **Anton, the only reason we have safety systems around here is because managers want to cover their arse.**

Mate, I think there might be a bit more to it than that.

Just remember that safety systems can also be used by employees to keep themselves safe – to cover their own arse, so to speak.

This belief can be formed when there appears to be an over abundance of safety systems or when safety systems are implemented following an incident or injury.

It is true that managers have a responsibility to comply with a range of workplace health and safety regulations and it is incumbent on them to make sure that the company provides a safe workplace and safe systems of work. But, I really don't think that legal obligation is the only reason that there are safety systems on site.

Managers don't want to see anyone get hurt at work – just as you don't. Imagine how you would feel if you found out that one of your workmates had been badly injured at work. You would feel terrible and managers feel that pain too. They don't want to see anyone get hurt anymore than you do. It is a tragedy for everyone in the company when an employee is injured.

Managers feel responsible for your safety, and they will support you to make your job safer. It is sometimes hard to believe that, but it is the truth. How do I know; because I have been in management roles before, and I know how much responsibility I took for the safety of those that reported to me!

When someone is injured at work, it is the manager who has to make the phone calls to the loved ones and support the family during the difficult times that follow. It is generally the manager that addresses the workmates of the injured worker and answers the hard questions relating to the causes of the incident. Managers have a tough role, but following an incident, it is even tougher. Now, I am not saying that managers are always right, but I do know that they care for their employees enough to want them to work safely. Not so that they can comply with regulations, but so that their employees can leave work at the end of each day without having been harmed or hurt. We all want that for our workmates.

> *So mate, managers are like you, they just don't want to see anyone get hurt at work. They are not covering their arse; they are trying to prevent injuries.*

CHAPTER 16

> **“** *Anton, if I work safely, my team members think I'm stupid and ridicule me.* **”**

Mate, I understand that on some crews, this can be an issue. It is called peer pressure, and it is no different to what used to occur in the school yard when your mates pressured you to have a smoke or to miss a class.

Some of your workmates won't support the fact that you are engaged in the safety process, and that you are willing to take the time to work safely. They will think that you are a 'kiss arse' or they will think that you are not one of the 'team', not one of the boys. In their minds, safety is a waste of time, because they know their jobs, and they don't need any paperwork to help them to work safely. They don't get hurt at work, and all the paperwork only makes it harder, and slower, to get their job done.

So they ridicule you for taking a stand; for being the odd one out who wears personal protective equipment (PPE) or takes a few minutes at the start of the job to identify hazards. You might even try to have a meaningful safety discussion, though some employees can't see the value in what you are doing.

The challenge for you is to maintain your vigilance and willingness to work safely despite the ridicule and potential ostracism from the team. You must stay focused on why you work safety in the first place – so that you can finish each work day without injury. If your workmates don't share the same commitment to their own safety that must not distract you. The more strongly you stay safety focused, the more chance you will have of changing the attitudes and opinions of your workmates. Not to mention the fact that you are less likely to get injured at work.

It is disappointing that there are still employees that show a lack of tolerance towards those in their teams or crews that are willing to take the time to put safety first. It is one thing to have an unsafe attitude, but it is completely another to make other people feel inadequate because they have a different attitude towards workplace safety.

*So mate, don't let peer pressure or
ridicule dissuade you from working safely
and committing to staying safe at work.
Remember that it is your attitude and
mindset will keep you from getting injured.*

CHAPTER 17

> **Anton, it is just great when I have to do some work at home; I don't have to do all the safety stuff, can just hop in and get it done!**

Mate, I hear that a lot. Like the guy that explained to me that you should wear undies while you are welding at home in your footy shorts because you can suffer, as he did, flash burns to your genitals. This is very painful he explained during a safety session on a mine site. But, why don't you take safety home, and work as safely at home as you do at work.

Generally, what people share with me is that they will take safety home, but only when it is possible for one of their family to get hurt. For example, if something, like pool chemicals or lawn mowing, could harm their children or their signifi cant other, they take all possible precautions to make sure that no-one gets hurt. Again, like in chapter 8, it is alright if they hurt themselves, as they are the only one injured (or so they think).

An important thing to consider here is the type of example you are setting for your family when they see you working safely only when they are around you. Remember, other people take your lead and follow your example from watching how you behave.

Another thing to consider is that, more than most people in your neighborhood, you have all of the skills and knowledge of how to work safely. You might even have all the PPE that you need at home, as well as at work. So, there is really no excuse for you to not work safely at home. It is just that you think it is too much trouble and that because there are no bosses at home and no set procedures to follow; it is alright to take a few extra risks.

Mate, you would be surprised to learn just how many incidents and injuries occur in the home, and how many of those were totally preventable.

> *So mate, just because you are not at work; don't forget to think about safety at home, too. You can get injured just as badly at home as you can at work. Plus, others are watching and you want to be a good example, don't you?*

CHAPTER 18

> **" Anton, where to from
> here? How can I apply some of the
> things we have been discussing? "**

Mate, that's easy. Why don't you write down a safety choice goal that you can follow through on, and that will allow you to apply something that you have learnt from this discussion.

You may choose a goal that you have been thinking about for a while, or you might choose a goal that you were prompted to think about during our discussion.

The most important thing about setting a safety choice goal, though, is following through on it. Don't just write it down, but make sure you take some action.

Following our discussion, my safety choice goals, are:

....

....

....

....

....

....

....

....

....

....

....

....

....

CHAPTER 19

> **"** *Anton, thanks for the chat.* **"**
> *How else can I apply the information*
> *that we have discussed?*

Well mate, it has been great chatting with you. Thank you for being so honest with your questions and comments, and I hope I have been able to respond to them clarity and relevance.

Look, there is no reason for you not to work safely and to end each work day in the same condition that you started it.

Have a safe day, and if you would like to continue this chat, feel free to contact me at:

www.theguineagroup.com.au
info@ theguineagroup.com.au

In relation to using this book, there are fi ve ways that you can use it to make a difference to your safety at work, and they are:

1. You can apply the lessons from each chapter,

2. You can also examine your safety attitude, and if you need to, change it, in order to prevent yourself from being injured at work (I consider myself very lucky to have had such a serious accident when and how I did – I was very unsafe, and it was only a matter of time until I hurt myself – I am lucky I was not killed. I learnt a lot from that incident, and you can learn from it also),

3. You can use some of the chapters as discussion points at toolbox talks or safety meetings. Flesh out the real issues, and instead of using safe lifting methods or the other general safety topics, challenge your fellow employees to share their views about the issues that are raised in this book,

4. You can help us to collect stories of 'safety belief busters'. These are stories from employees that show how the safety beliefs, such as those mentioned in this book, can be busted. I have included some safety belief busters as examples

(email your stories to info@letstalkaboutsafety.
com.au),

5. You can follow through on the one or more
    safety choice goals that you made. You can do
    something to make your workplace safer. You
    might even like to discuss your safety choice goals
    with your workmates. Why don't you ask them
    how they are going with their goals?

SAFETY BELIEF BUSTERS

How to break away from those old safety beliefs

I recently visited a mine site, where I was conducting safety sessions for employees on the topic of how to be more risk mindful. About half way through the session, one employee shared his experience, and his thoughts, on a zero incident workplace. He believed that shit just happened. The employee commented that, two years earlier, he would never have believed that achieving zero incidents was possible. When his work crew started working towards zero harm, they struggled, though finally they went for one month with zero incidents. Then, they managed to go for 12 months with zero incidents. At the time we had this discussion, the employee's team had gone for two years without an incident. That was not only an amazing achievement, but one that changed the belief of the employee in relation to zero incidents. He commented that he is now a firm believer in the concept, and knows that it is not only achievable, but also sustainable. *He has changed his belief.*

During one of my very first safety presentations, one of the employees in attendance (who happened to be an Electrician) approached me after the session. He had commented during the session that he was not surprised that I had used a steel ruler in a switchboard, as once the board was isolated, that should be safe enough to do. "You should never get injured doing that" he had said. The electrician also said that he regularly used a steel tape measure in switchboards to measure where components or cabling would be mounted. Then, I showed him the results of the burns that I had suffered. He commented after the session that he thought an incident would never happen to him. He also commented that he would never use a steel tape measure in a switchboard again. *Another belief busted.*

Some of the most important safety belief busters are those that are related to taking safety home. It is regularly that I get asked how people can teach their kids about safety. My response is generally focused on leading by example, and demonstrating through your actions how to act safely. I had a discussion with someone recently, and I was told "Anton, the answer is a very simple one, there is nothing complicated about it; you just need to talk about it at home". Most of us don't. When was the last time that you talked to your kids about safety? I certainly believed that as parents, we just kept our kids from doing crazy stuff and ensured that we showed them what is safe. I certainly never considered how important some direct conversations about safety could be to my kid's education. *Another belief busted.*

THANKS AND ACKNOWLEDGEMENTS

Without you all, this would not be possible

There are always many people to thank for their contribution to a book, and in this case the fi rst group of people that I want to thank is the workers all over the world that I have worked with, spoken for and just chatted with. Your insight into the safety arena is always fascinating and interesting.

Many thanks go to Marc McLaren, who has been a source of inspiration, guidance and friendship. Marc has been a mentor and running partner, and I enjoy thoroughly the time that we spend together. Needless to say that it is always a learning experience.

Thank you to James Wood, who allowed me to use his story as part of this book. He is an outstanding individual, who reminds me that things are never as bad as they seem.

Thank you to the book editor, Ian Grinblat, who completed the editing within days. Yvette Adams was just amazing as a designer, and without her, this book would not look as good as it does and it would not have been ready for distribution as quickly as it was. Shaun Ford was responsible for getting the book printed. He was amazing to work with, also. Pete Demamiel, at Internet Brokers, is always the brains behind my web site creation and development.

Finally, and most of all, thanks to my wonderful family, Julie, Toby and Zac. Julie spent much time sitting in intensive care, and then the burns unit, waiting for me to heal, and for that I am indebted. Toby and Zac are growing up quickly, and Toby wants to be a Structural Engineer. I hope he stays safe at work. Zac is not sure yet, but mum and dad will be there for him, regardless of his life's choices.

If I have missed someone, I apologize.

ABOUT THE AUTHOR

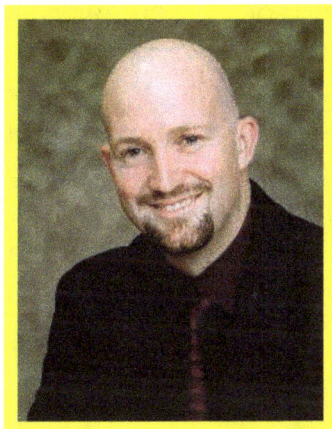

Anton Guinea is energetic and inspirational. He builds rapport instantly, and motivates all who have had the pleasure of hearing him speak publicly. He has spoken both in Australia, and overseas, and he is internationally recognised as an outstanding motivational speaker.

Anton, the son of a school teacher and a safety offcer, was born and bred in Gladstone, Queensland, Australia. He completed his schooling, and then an apprenticeship as an electrician. He worked as a tradesman for only three years, before be began a swift climb through the organisational structures of several of Australia's major employers. He is achieving his career goals, and more, and is able to assist others to generate similar drive and ambition to do the same. Anton is also a results coach. He helps people achieve their goals in life. Find out more at www.yourresultscoach.com.au.

Anton has overcome signifi cant adversity in his life, such as a near death electrical accident that results in severe burns. His schooling days were what he describes as miserable failures and in his early thirties his weight was 20 kilograms higher than it should have been. His achievements are testimonial to his courage, spirit and never failing determination to reach his greatest potential in life. You will be inspired by his approach to life, his ability to motivate and his willingness to share all that he has learnt and experienced with those who are equally driven to succeed.

Success in his personal life has also been important for Anton, and he shares his success with his wife of 15 years, Julie, and their two boys, Tobias and Zachary.

Anton's fi rst book was titled "Give Your Life Direction", and is previewed below:

This book is an outstanding example of what is possible in life. It is told by Anton Guinea, who has changed his life by changing his thinking and his attitude. Anton uses both his own unique story, and the story of his 'two mates' who have both managed to achieve outstanding results after being overcome by adversity. Terrible burns injuries and extreme academic failures were not enough to stop Anton's two mates (Paul and Gary) from producing the results that most of the population only dream about.

Follow the story of these two outstanding personalities, and live the journey that they have undertaken to right the wrongs of their past, and fi nally become the men that they were always capable of being.

This book is not only an engaging story about how altering your thinking, your focus and your belief system can change your life instantly, but it is also full of great ideas and strategies to allow you to achieve the same success as Anton and his two mates. Be inspired by their stories of bravery, courage and determination, and apply the same successful life improvement concepts and strategies in your own life.

More information on Anton and his motivational products can be found at:

www.theguineagroup.com.au
Email Anton on: info@ theguineagroup.com.au

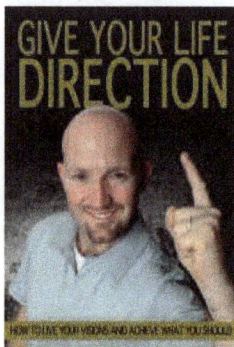

**Give Your Life
Direction**
- Book

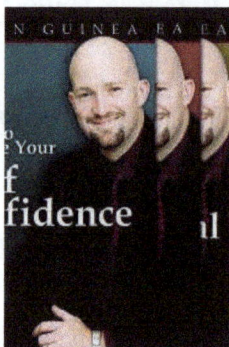

**Anton Guinea
Program Set**
- CDs

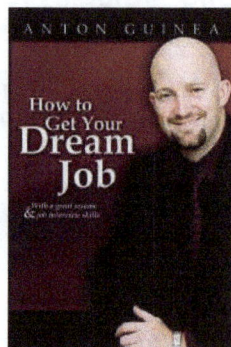

**How to Get Your
Dream Job**
- CD

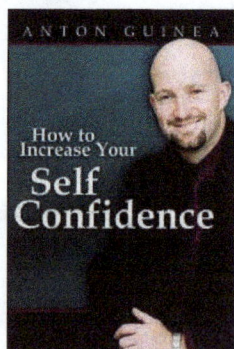

**How to Increase
Your Self
Confidence**
- CD

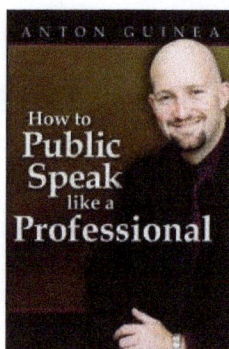

**How to Public
Speak Like a
Professional**
- CD

BIBLIOGRAPHY

Give Your Life Direction:
www.giveyourlifedirection.com.au